The Catholic Mother's Traditional Lenten Journal

by

Mrs. Leane VanderPutten

ISBN-13:
978-1974317448

ISBN-10:
1974317447

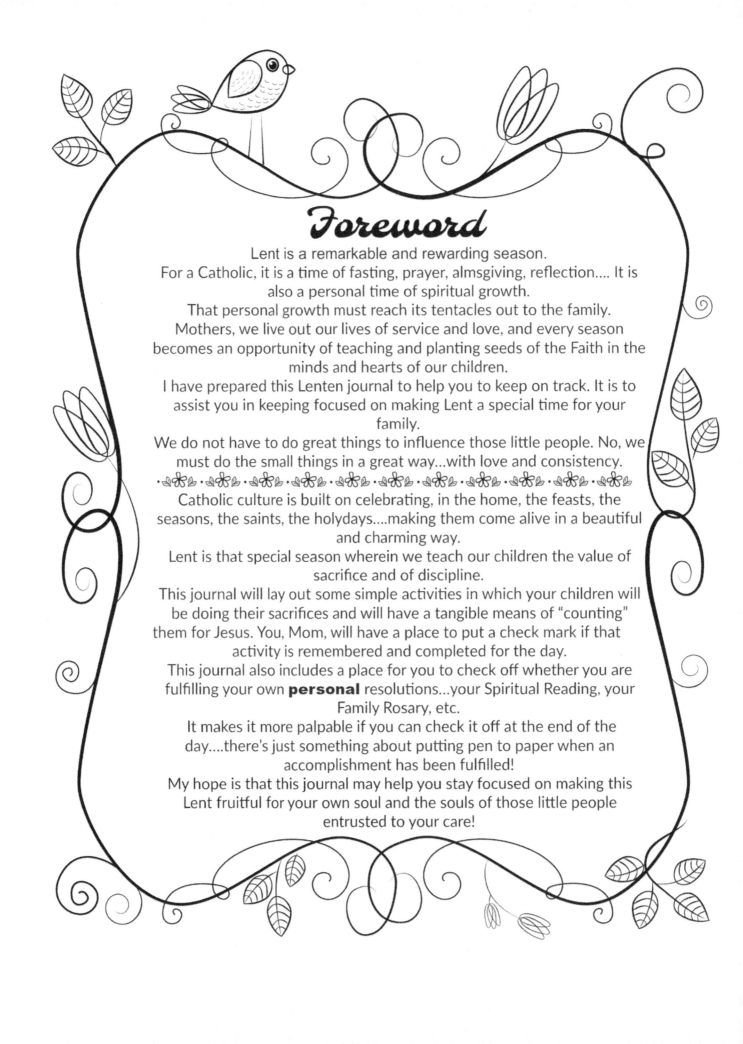

Foreword

Lent is a remarkable and rewarding season.
For a Catholic, it is a time of fasting, prayer, almsgiving, reflection.... It is also a personal time of spiritual growth.
That personal growth must reach its tentacles out to the family.
Mothers, we live out our lives of service and love, and every season becomes an opportunity of teaching and planting seeds of the Faith in the minds and hearts of our children.
I have prepared this Lenten journal to help you to keep on track. It is to assist you in keeping focused on making Lent a special time for your family.
We do not have to do great things to influence those little people. No, we must do the small things in a great way...with love and consistency.

Catholic culture is built on celebrating, in the home, the feasts, the seasons, the saints, the holydays....making them come alive in a beautiful and charming way.
Lent is that special season wherein we teach our children the value of sacrifice and of discipline.
This journal will lay out some simple activities in which your children will be doing their sacrifices and will have a tangible means of "counting" them for Jesus. You, Mom, will have a place to put a check mark if that activity is remembered and completed for the day.
This journal also includes a place for you to check off whether you are fulfilling your own **personal** resolutions...your Spiritual Reading, your Family Rosary, etc.
It makes it more palpable if you can check it off at the end of the day....there's just something about putting pen to paper when an accomplishment has been fulfilled!
My hope is that this journal may help you stay focused on making this Lent fruitful for your own soul and the souls of those little people entrusted to your care!

Lenten Activities

Lenten Beans

A great activity for Lent is the Lima Beans for sacrifices!
The beginning of Lent each child has their own pile of different colored lima beans (they can color them with markers or paint) so they can differentiate from each other's beans. Every time a sacrifice is made they will put one of their own lima beans in the jar. When Easter comes the number of lima beans is rewarded accordingly.
A Variation: Use any type of bean, each child adding to the jar as sacrifices (extra prayers, etc.) are accomplished and at the end of the Lenten season, the beans are replaced with jelly beans and divided equally amongst the children.

A sweet practice that will be fondly remembered by the kids as they grow into adulthood….

> Living in a fallen world, our children are bound to be hurt, both physically and spiritually.
> We will save them years of wasted opportunities if we teach them that, along with everything else, pain is part of their prayer.
> -Mary Reed Newland

Crown of Thorns Activity #1

The Crown of Thorns Lenten Activity is a beautiful way to symbolize Our Lord's sufferings and provides a way for children to visualize comforting Him in His pain…
There are two ways to do this.
One is to make an actual *Crown of Thorns* out of a salt and flour dough mixture.

Materials:
4 c. flour
1 c. salt
Water
Toothpicks

Directions:
Mix flour and salt. Mix enough warm water to make a stiff dough. Knead until smooth. Roll three long ropes and loosely braid them. Form braid into a circle and stick toothpicks loosely throughout the entire crown. Bake at 350° F for an hour or until it is dry and light brown. (You may substitute some brewed coffee for the water to make the crown a darker color. You can also brush some egg whites on the Crown before you bake it to produce a shiny effect.)
Put the Crown in a prominent place; put a purple piece of material under it, if you wish.
For each Lenten sacrifice, the children put a small silk flower on each of the toothpicks. Because the toothpicks fill up quickly, we tell the children that 3 small sacrifices or one big sacrifice equals a flower.
By Easter, the Crown of Thorns is an array of beauty!
*Note: Another way to use this Crown of Thorns is to fill the unbaked Crown with toothpicks (don't put them in too far or they won't come out easily) and as the children do their sacrifices, they pull a toothpick **out!** The goal is to have all the "thorns" removed by *Easter.* The children can then decorate the Crown with flowers, glitter, beads, paint, etc. It may used be used as an **Easter centerpiece!**

Crown of Thorns Activity #2

The other way to do this activity is to **draw** the *Crown of Thorns* on a big poster board. (Make sure you start the season off with lots of different colored markers!)

The children will **draw** the flowers on each thorn as they do the sacrifices. It is very interesting to see the unique blossoms that grow on each thorn!

We posted our *Crown of Thorns* on the refrigerator for all to see. By Easter, it was an artistic array of beauty!

Other Activities

The Cross - Another activity that can be used to show the sacrifices the children make is a large cross made out of posterboard. The children can cut out flowers (or use a punch) and glue them on the cross for the sacrifices. Each child can have a different color of construction paper. Small crosses could take the place of the flowers.

Good Friday

From: Around the Year With the Trapp Family by Maria von Trapp

Good Friday is a very quiet day with us.

There is little to do in the kitchen, since fasting is observed rigorously on this day.

We have no breakfast, and all that is served for lunch, on a bare table without tablecloth, is one pot of thick soup, "Einbrennsuppe," which everyone eats standing up in silence. There is little noise around the house. Talking is restricted to the bare essentials, as it would be if a dearly beloved was lying dead in the house. As we are so privileged as to have a chapel in our house, we use the day when the holy house of God is empty and desolate to clean and polish all the sacred vessels and chalices and the ciborium, the monstrance, candlesticks, and censer.

The vigil light before the picture of the Blessed Mother in the living room is also extinguished, because on Good Friday Christ, the Light of the World, is dead.

From twelve until three, the hours of Our Lord's agony on the cross, all activity stops. We sit together in the empty chapel before the cross and spend these hours in prayer, meditation, and spiritual reading. From time to time we rise and sing one or the other of the beautiful Lenten hymns and motets.

From: The Year and Our Family by Mary Reed Newland

For the hours spent at home by those who cannot get to the rites of Good Friday, it is good to plan special activities in order to help all keep a spirit of recollection. With many little children, silence is almost impossible, but as they grow older, they begin to cooperate.

Friends of ours have had their children make a Resurrection Garden (see next page) outdoors, separately, on Good Friday. They used whatever they could find at hand – stones, mosses, sticks, acorns.

A drawing project will keep Peter occupied. Having said the Stations of the Cross during Lent, he applies himself seriously to illustrating them.

Rereading the passages about the Passion will keep another child busy, read out of Scripture or from a favorite life of Christ.

For a boy who is fidgety and must be active, a solitary chore that is a penance is better: perhaps cleaning the goat stalls or spreading hay and manure from the goose's pen on the garden.

I know many mothers who, because they must be at home with their babies during this time, save a task that especially tries them.

Each has his or her way of best spending the hours of Good Friday, but it will work out most successfully if the program for the day is well planned.

Perhaps one of the tasks for several of the children can be copying Psalm 21 to be used at night prayers this evening. Our Lord quoted the first line of it from the Cross. It prophesied Christ's Passion and Death and our salvation: "My God, my God, why have You forsaken me...."

This was the great prayer of our Lord on the Cross. The family may divide itself and read the lines alternately.

Hot Cross Buns!

Ingredients:

12 tablespoons (1 1/2 sticks) butter, melted and cooled
1 cup plus 1 tablespoon milk
2 packages yeast
1/2 cup sugar
2 teaspoons salt
3/4 teaspoon cinnamon
1/2 teaspoon nutmeg
4 large eggs, lightly beaten
5 1/2 cups flour
1 1/3 cups currants or raisins
1 large egg white
2 cups confectioners' sugar
2 tablespoons freshly squeezed lemon juice

Hot Cross Buns, with their combination of spicy, sweet and fruity flavors have long been an Easter tradition, with the pastry cross on top of the buns symbolising and reminding Christians of the cross that Jesus was killed upon...

Directions:

Heat 1 cup milk until it is warm.

Pour warm milk into the bowl. Add yeast, sugar, 2 teaspoons salt, melted butter, cinnamon, nutmeg, and beaten eggs and mix with whisk or mixer.

Add flour, 1 cup at a time, until a soft, slightly sticky dough forms. Continue kneading until smooth. Add currants, and knead until combined.

Turn dough out onto a heavily floured surface. Knead to evenly distribute currants, about 1 minute.

Shape dough into a ball, and place in the buttered bowl; turn ball to coat with butter, and cover bowl tightly with plastic wrap. Let dough rise in a warm place until doubled in bulk, about 1 hour 20 minutes.

Shape dough into balls and place on buttered baking sheet, 1/2 inch apart. Cover and let rise in warm place to double in bulk. (About 1 hour)

Heat oven to 375 degrees, with rack positioned in center.

To make egg wash, whisk together egg white, 1 tablespoon water, and pinch of salt in a small bowl; brush tops of buns with egg wash. Using very sharp scissors or a buttered slicing knife, slice a cross into the top of each bun.

Transfer pan to oven, and bake until golden brown, about 25 minutes.

Make glaze: In a medium bowl, whisk together 1 tablespoon milk, confectioner's sugar, and lemon juice. Spoon glaze over buns and serve. Yum!

Easter!

The Resurrection Garden: The garden is made of simple outdoor materials to represent the empty tomb and the unoccupied crosses. Stones, moss, branches, etc. are gathered up and placed in the garden. It is a beautiful symbol of Our Lord's resurrection and the children will enjoy making it special!

The Most Beautiful Easter Story!
From The Year and Our Lord by Mary Reed Newland

This is, for me, the most beautiful of all the Easter stories.

It should be the very last thing at night, after prayers, for the little ones. Ours have heard it as they lay in their beds.

It is about Mary Magdalene and how she found Him in the garden on Easter morning. She did not really understand. After all He had said about rising on the third day, still she wept and wrung her hands and looked for Him.

Even when she saw the angels, it did not dawn on her. Then – she saw Jesus. Thinking He was a gardener, she heard Him say, "Woman, why art thou weeping? For whom art thou searching?"

And she said, "If it is thou, Sir, that hast carried Him off, tell me where thou hast put Him, and I will take Him away."

Then that lovely moment. He said simply, "Mary." And she knew.

How tender, the love that inspired them to record this scene. We know that He appeared to His Mother first. It is an ancient tradition in the Church, and St. Teresa of Avila and many others confirm it.

But for us who are sinners, the scene described so carefully is this meeting with the one who was such a great sinner. It should be a part of every child's Easter Eve, and often it will make them weep.

But these are fine, good tears, that come because they understand that He loves them.

Resolutions

My Lenten Resolutions

Okay, here goes! Here's where the rubber meets the road! We need to take some time and thought to decide what we are adding in, giving up, or what we will try to change this Lent. All sacrifice, when done for the right reasons, is a powerful prayer and a means of detaching ourselves from the world. Don't bite off more than you can chew! The sacrifices don't have to be great but those we choose need to be done with consistency and perseverance, picking ourselves up when we fall.

Personal Resolutions

(Some examples: Fasting, giving up coffee, salt or other food or drinks, adding some doable prayers, no complaining, no snooze button, etc.)

Family Resolutions

(Some examples: Extra Religious reading, no movies, no listening to music, giving money to the poor, daily Mass, etc.)

Remember: We are making resolutions to grow in love of Our Lord and our fellow man. Mothers, if giving up coffee causes you to be very cranky with your family, pick something else! You don't want *others* to suffer from **your** resolutions! You can especially focus on doing something extra, instead of giving up something. Use prudence, especially if you are pregnant or nursing.

The Rosary

Although not a specific Lenten custom, the daily Rosary will be included in your checklist each day. If you don't get anything else done from the list for that day, but you are able to put a checkmark by the Rosary, you have done the most important thing!

"The Rosary is a powerful weapon to put the demons to flight and to keep oneself from sin…If you desire peace in your hearts, in your homes, and in your country, assemble each evening to recite the Rosary. Let not even one day pass without saying it, no matter how burdened you may be with many cares and labors." – Pope Pius XI

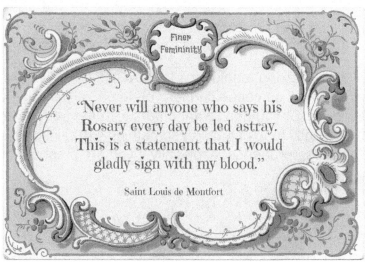

Finer Femininity

"Never will anyone who says his Rosary every day be led astray. This is a statement that I would gladly sign with my blood."

Saint Louis de Montfort

*"**There is also the question of time.**
Where do we find the time to participate in the **Church's liturgical year** with our children?
Like these other questions, the answer is, **we can find it if we plan for it.**
We can find it quite easily by looking to see where we waste it.
Not wasting it is not easy, because the habits of time-wasting, although they are harmless, are hard to break – as I know from experience.
Mothers have this struggle all to themselves. It involves such things as the radio (now internet) habit, coffee breaks, long telephone conversations, chatting with neighbors, a heavy involvement in outside activities.
Somewhere most American women CAN "find time" to devote to the **enriching of their families' spiritual life.**
The joyous discovery is that once we have struggled and found the time, **tasted and seen how sweet are these pursuits together,** we begin to gauge all our doings so that there will be time – because we are convinced **there must be.**"*
-Mary Reed Newland, The Year and Our Children

Your Journal

Ash Wednesday

My Cross I Wish to Thank God for Today:

_____

_____

The Person or Situation I am Offering it for:

_____

_____

Something Special that Happened Today:

_____

_____

_____

_____

Your Daily Lenten Checklist:

Did you accomplish it today?
Bravo! Put a check in the heart!

Daily Resolutions Fulfilled.......................... ♡

Spiritual Reading.............................. ♡

Children's Activity.......................... ♡

Daily Rosary............................ ♡
Additional Items:

_____ ♡

_____ ♡

Quote:

In these weeks of the Lenten season, the mother of the family has much to teach her children. She will introduce them to the meaning of the color of violet in church. She will prepare them for the forty sacred days of retreat, and will help them to formulate their Lenten resolutions, which should be written on a sheet of paper and placed on the house altar.
-Maria von Trapp

Thursday after Ash Wednesday

Three Things I am Grateful for Today:

1. _____

2. _____

3. _____

Something Special that Happened Today:

_____

_____

_____

_____

Your Daily Lenten Checklist:

Did you accomplish it today?
Bravo! Put a check in the heart!

Daily Resolutions Fulfilled.........................

Spiritual Reading...................................

Children's Activity.................................

Daily Rosary.......................................
Additional Items:

_____

_____

Quote:

It is important that Lenten resolutions do not use the negative approach only, such as, "I won't do this" and "I won't do that."

They should start positively, with "I will use these three books" (this as soon as the child can read); "I will use the time I save by abstaining from television for this and this...." "I will use the money I save by not going to the movies for alms given to...."
-Maria von Trapp

Friday after Ash Wednesday

Personal Prayer Intention for Today:

_____

_____

_____

Something Special that Happened Today:

_____

_____

_____

_____

Your Daily Lenten Checklist:

Did you accomplish it today?
Bravo! Put a check in the heart!

Daily Resolutions Fulfilled...........................

Spiritual Reading................................

Children's Activity.........................

Daily Rosary.........................
Additional Items:

_____

_____

Quote:

It is worth while now for me, – now while the brief occasion lasts – to overcome one temptation, to do one small kindness, to improve my mind by one half hour of study, to wait in patience when there is nothing else to be done, to bear a headache, or sleeplessness, or some small pain.

It is always worth while doing the good that just at this moment lies within my power to do.

Saturday after Ash Wednesday

My Cross I Wish to Thank God for Today:

_____

_____

The Person or Situation I am Offering it for:

_____

_____

Something Special that Happened Today:

_____

_____

_____

_____

Your Daily Lenten Checklist:

Did you accomplish it today?
Bravo! Put a check in the heart!

Daily Resolutions Fulfilled.........................

Spiritual Reading.............................

Children's Activity...........................

Daily Rosary.........................
Additional Items:

_____

_____

Quote:

If we feel that it is unnatural to ask penances of children while they are still very young – penances within their reach – we forget that self-denial must be learned very young, that it is the forming of character, that the very grace of their Baptism flows from the Cross.
- Mary Reed Newland

Monday of the First Week in Lent

Three Things I am Grateful for Today:

1. _____
2. _____
3. _____

Something Special that Happened Today:

_____

_____

_____

_____

Your Daily Lenten Checklist:

Did you accomplish it today?
Bravo! Put a check in the heart!

Daily Resolutions Fulfilled..........................

Spiritual Reading...............................

Children's Activity...........................

Daily Rosary...........................
Additional Items:

_____

_____

Quote:

It is our business, we who are husbands and wives and children, we who are family and home people—it is our business to "Christize" ourselves and our houses and our neighborhoods. That is the business that we ought to be about. If we were about it as we ought to be, gradually we would Christize all the world; we would create world peace; we would disarm and harmonize the nations.
-Joseph Breig

Tuesday of the First Week in Lent

Personal Prayer Intention for Today:

_____

_____

_____

Something Special that Happened Today:

_____

_____

_____

_____

Your Daily Lenten Checklist:

Did you accomplish it today?
Bravo! Put a check in the heart!

Daily Resolutions Fulfilled.......................... ♡

Spiritual Reading.......................... ♡

Children's Activity.......................... ♡

Daily Rosary.......................... ♡
Additional Items:

_____ ♡

_____ ♡

Quote:

"The very presence of a woman who knows how to combine an enlightened piety with mildness, tact, and thoughtful sympathy, is a constant sermon; she speaks by her very silence, she instills convictions without argument, she attracts souls without wounding susceptibilities; and both in her own house and in her dealings with men and things, she plays the part of the soft cotton wool we put between precious but fragile vases to prevent their mutually injuring each other."
-Msgr Landriot

Wednesday of the First Week in Lent

My Cross I Wish to Thank God for Today:

_____

_____

The Person or Situation I am Offering it for:

_____

_____

Something Special that Happened Today:

_____

_____

_____

_____

Your Daily Lenten Checklist:

Did you accomplish it today?
Bravo! Put a check in the heart!

Daily Resolutions Fulfilled........................... ♡

Spiritual Reading................................. ♡

Children's Activity............................. ♡

Daily Rosary......................... ♡
Additional Items

_____ ♡

_____ ♡

Quote:

My God, since You agreed to free me and to heal me on the one condition that I show You, with tears of sorrow, my faults and weaknesses; since, O Lord, my soul is sick, I bring to You all my sins and misfortunes.
There is no sin, no weakness of soul or mind for which You do not have an adequate remedy, purchased by Your death.
All my salvation and joy are in You, O Crucified Christ, and in whatever state I happen to be, I shall never take my eyes away from Your Cross." –St. Angela of Foligno

Thursday of the First Week in Lent

Three Things I am Grateful for Today:

1. _____

2. _____

3. _____

Something Special that Happened Today:

_____

_____

_____

_____

Your Daily Lenten Checklist:

Did you accomplish it today?
Bravo! Put a check in the heart!

Daily Resolutions Fulfilled............................ ♡

Spiritual Reading.. ♡

Children's Activity...................................... ♡

Daily Rosary.. ♡
Additional Items:

_____

_____

Quote:

The Christian concept of carrying the Cross is simply a nutshell description of an honest, mature and religious outlook on life. It is a simple fact that even the longest life is short. Even the most poignant sorrow is comparatively brief. The truth is that life and everything in life are merely means to an end, to a purpose, to an achievement. And the achievement is nothing short of an eternity of such happiness as cannot possibly be described because it is far beyond the power of the human mind to realize or to imagine.
—Joseph Breig, A Family's Way of the Cross

Friday of the First Week in Lent

Personal Prayer Intention for Today:

_____

_____

_____

Something Special that Happened Today:

_____

_____

_____

_____

Your Daily Lenten Checklist:

Did you accomplish it today?
Bravo! Put a check in the heart!

Daily Resolutions Fulfilled............................ ♡

Spiritual Reading.. ♡

Children's Activity...................................... ♡

Daily Rosary... ♡
Additional Items:

_____ ♡

_____ ♡

Quote:

In the state of grace and with the right intention, married people can become saints doing their everyday home work.

They often gain more graces with a dish cloth, as one may sometime gain more graces getting up in the middle of the night to care for a baby than spending an hour in church. It is a matter of doing the right thing at the right time. Yes, but even more, it is fulfilling a Sacramental vocation.
-Joseph Breig, The Family and the Cross, 1950's

Saturday of the First Week in Lent

My Cross I Wish to Thank God for Today:

_____

_____

The Person or Situation I am Offering it for:

_____

_____

Something Special that Happened Today:

_____

_____

_____

_____

Your Daily Lenten Checklist:

Did you accomplish it today?
Bravo! Put a check in the heart!

Daily Resolutions Fulfilled........................ ♡

Spiritual Reading................................. ♡

Children's Activity............................... ♡

Daily Rosary..................................... ♡
Additional Items:

_____ ♡

_____

Quote:

Not all can see the value of suffering. Suffering is often so inward, so hard to articulate. It has been a special mystery to all, especially pagans. Their many explanations have never been satisfactory.

A good Catholic makes friends with pain. He holds God's gifts close to himself but always with open hands. When God allows us sufferings it is not to do us harm but to gather us into His arms.
-The Family and the Cross, Joseph Breig

Monday of the
Second Week of Lent

Three Things I am Grateful
for Today:

1. _____

2. _____

3. _____

Something Special that Happened Today:

_____

_____

_____

_____

Your Daily Lenten Checklist:

Did you accomplish it today?
Bravo! Put a check in the heart!

Daily Resolutions Fulfilled............................ ♡

Spiritual Reading................................. ♡

Children's Activity........................... ♡

Daily Rosary................................. ♡
Additional Items:

_____ ♡

_____ ♡

Quote:

Lent is a precious time, a time for the mother to introduce her children to the three ancient good works–prayer, fasting, and giving of alms–with which we can atone for our sins. It will take root in young hearts, never to be forgotten.
-Maria von Trapp

Tuesday of the Second Week in Lent

Personal Prayer Intention for Today:

_____

_____

_____

Something Special that Happened Today:

_____

_____

_____

_____

Your Daily Lenten Checklist:

Did you accomplish it today?
Bravo! Put a check in the heart!

Daily Resolutions Fulfilled............................

Spiritual Reading............................

Children's Activity............................

Daily Rosary............................
Additional Items:

_____

_____

Quote:

It should be absolutely unbearable to us to think that there are thousands of people around us who pride themselves on rigorous feats of fast and abstinence for motives as flimsy as good looks, while we cannot bring ourselves to give up a bare minimum.
-Maria von Trapp

Wednesday of the Second Week in Lent

My Cross I Wish to Thank God for Today:

_____

_____

The Person or Situation I am Offering it for:

_____

_____

Something Special that Happened Today:

_____

_____

_____

_____

Your Daily Lenten Checklist:

Did you accomplish it today?
Bravo! Put a check in the heart!

Daily Resolutions Fulfilled.......................... ♡

Spiritual Reading............................... ♡

Children's Activity........................... ♡

Daily Rosary..................... ♡
Additional Items

_____ ♡

_____ ♡

Quote:

You can make your greatest contribution to your family as the heart of your home—not its head. From you, your children should learn to love others and to give of themselves unstintingly in the spirit of sacrifice. Never underestimate the importance of your role. For upon you depends the emotional growth of your children, and such growth will better prepare them to live happy and holy lives than any amount of intellectual training they may receive.

Rev. George Kelly, Catholic Family Handbook

Thursday of the Second Week in Lent

Three Things I am Grateful for Today:

1. _____

2. _____

3. _____

Something Special that Happened Today:

_____

_____

_____

_____

Your Daily Lenten Checklist:

Did you accomplish it today?
Bravo! Put a check in the heart!

Daily Resolutions Fulfilled..........................

Spiritual Reading..............................

Children's Activity..........................

Daily Rosary...........................
Additional Items:

_____

_____

Quote:

Even so, O Woman, within that world which is your home and kingdom, your face is to light up and brighten and beautify all things, and your heart is to be the source of that vital fire and strength without which the father can be no true father, the brother no true brother, the sister no true sister, since all have to learn from you how to love, how to labor lovingly, how to be forgetful of self, and mindful only of the welfare of others.
-Rev. Bernard O'Reilly, 1894

Friday of the
Second Week in Lent

Personal Prayer Intention for Today:

_____

_____

_____

Something Special that Happened Today:

_____

_____

_____

_____

Your Daily Lenten Checklist:

Did you accomplish it today?
Bravo! Put a check in the heart!

Daily Resolutions Fulfilled...........................

Spiritual Reading................................

Children's Activity..............................

Daily Rosary................................
Additional Items

_____

_____

Quote:

The Christian family will not be restored, nor will it be maintained, without the restoration and the maintenance of Christian practices—the noblest practices surely, and the most obligatory, but likewise the most insignificant in appearance.

- Fr. Raoul Plus, S.J.,
Christ in the Home

Saturday of the
Second Week in Lent

My Cross I Wish to
Thank God for Today:

_____

_____

The Person or Situation I am
Offering it for:

_____

_____

_____

Something Special that Happened Today:

_____

_____

_____

_____

Your Daily Lenten Checklist:

Did you accomplish it today?
Bravo! Put a check in the heart!

Daily Resolutions Fulfilled............................

Spiritual Reading............................

Children's Activity............................

Daily Rosary............................
Additional Items:

_____

_____

Quote:

"Who shall blame a
child whose soul turns
eagerly to the noise and
distraction of
worldliness, if his
parents have failed to
show him that love and
peace and beauty are
found only in God?" -
Mary Reed Newland

Monday of the Third Week in Lent

Three Things I am Grateful for Today:

1. _____
2. _____
3. _____

Something Special that Happened Today:

_____

_____

_____

_____

Your Daily Lenten Checklist:

Did you accomplish it today? Bravo! Put a check in the heart!

Daily Resolutions Fulfilled......................... ♡

Spiritual Reading............................... ♡

Children's Activity............................. ♡

Daily Rosary........................... ♡
Additional Items

_____ ♡

_____ ♡

Quote:

"The Holy Family lived in a plain cottage among other working people, in a village perched on a hillside. Although they did not enjoy modern conveniences, the three persons who lived there made it the happiest home that ever was. You cannot imagine any of them at any time thinking first of himself. This is the kind of home a husband likes to return to and to remain in. Mary saw to it that such was their home. She took it as her career to be a successful homemaker and mother."
-Fr. Lawrence G. Lovasik

Tuesday of the Third Week in Lent

Personal Prayer Intention for Today:

_____

_____

_____

Something Special that Happened Today:

_____

_____

_____

_____

Your Daily Lenten Checklist:

Did you accomplish it today?
Bravo! Put a check in the heart!

Daily Resolutions Fulfilled...........................

Spiritual Reading.......................................

Children's Activity......................................

Daily Rosary..
Additional Items:

_____

_____

Quote:

"The Lord measures out perfection neither by the multitude nor the magnitude of our deeds, but by the manner in which we perform them."
– St. John of the Cross

Wednesday of the Third Week in Lent

My Cross I Wish to Thank God for Today:

_____

_____

The Person or Situation I am Offering it for:

_____

_____

Something Special that Happened Today:

_____

_____

_____

_____

Your Daily Lenten Checklist:

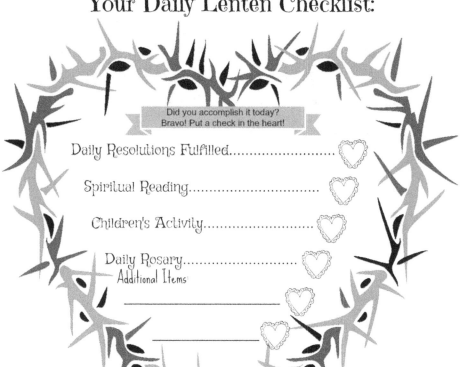

Did you accomplish it today? Bravo! Put a check in the heart!

Daily Resolutions Fulfilled.......................... ♡

Spiritual Reading.............................. ♡

Children's Activity.......................... ♡

Daily Rosary............................ ♡
Additional Items:

_____ ♡

_____ ♡

Quote:

"Pray, hope, and don't worry. Worry is useless, God is merciful and will hear your prayer."
St. Pio of Pietrelcina

Thursday of the Third Week in Lent

Three Things I am Grateful for Today:

1. _____
2. _____
3. _____

Something Special that Happened Today:

_____

_____

_____

_____

Your Daily Lenten Checklist:

Did you accomplish it today?
Bravo! Put a check in the heart!

Daily Resolutions Fulfilled..........................

Spiritual Reading................................

Children's Activity..........................

Daily Rosary............................
Additional Items:

_____

_____

Quote:

When you find your heart growing sad, divert yourself without a moment's delay; make a visit, enter into conversation with those around you, read some amusing book, take a walk, sing, do something, it matters not what, provided you close the door of your heart against this terrible enemy. As the sound of a trumpet gives the signal for a combat, so sad thoughts apprise the devil that a favorable moment has come for him to attack us.
-St. Francis de Sales

Friday of the Third Week in Lent

Personal Prayer Intention for Today:

_____

_____

_____

Something Special that Happened Today:

_____

_____

_____

_____

Your Daily Lenten Checklist:

Did you accomplish it today?
Bravo! Put a check in the heart!

Daily Resolutions Fulfilled............................ ♡

Spiritual Reading................................. ♡

Children's Activity................................ ♡

Daily Rosary.............................. ♡
Additional Items

_____

_____

Quote:

"In truth, the family circle is the nursery of saints. There the child finds the love, security and guidance which are his greatest needs. It is by loving and being loved that persons grow as persons. It is in the family that relationships are essentially personal and each person is valued as a person." – Dominican Sister, Australia, 1955

My Cross I Wish to
Thank God for Today:

_____

_____

The Person or Situation I am
Offering it for:

_____

_____

Something Special that Happened Today:

_____

_____

_____

_____

Your Daily Lenten Checklist:

Did you accomplish it today?
Bravo! Put a check in the heart!

Daily Resolutions Fulfilled..........................

Spiritual Reading..............................

Children's Activity..........................

Daily Rosary............................
Additional Items:

_____

_____

Quote:

"The Crucifix on the wall, the
pictures of Our Lord and His
Mother - the loveliest you
can afford - the little shrine
with lights and flowers -
these unceasingly speak to
your little ones of God's love
and His Beauty, preparing
them for that friendship with
God, that willing, personal
submission to Him that is
true freedom and happiness."
-Dominican Nun, Australia,
1955

Monday of the Fourth Week in Lent

Three Things I am Grateful for Today:

1. _____
2. _____
3. _____

Something Special that Happened Today:

_____

_____

_____

_____

Your Daily Lenten Checklist:

Did you accomplish it today?
Bravo! Put a check in the heart!

Daily Resolutions Fulfilled.......................... ♡

Spiritual Reading...................................... ♡

Children's Activity................................... ♡

Daily Rosary.. ♡
Additional Items:

_____ ♡

_____

Quote:

We have many institutions that we call schools, but the real schools where the real lessons of life are learned are our homes. –Fr. Lawrence Lovasik

It is good sometimes to know that although you have **sacrificed** many of the things modern "emancipated" women value so highly.....

your humble position is still the **proudest** in society.

–Fr. Lawrence Lovasik

Tuesday of the Fourth Week in Lent

Personal Prayer Intention for Today:

_____

_____

_____

Something Special that Happened Today:

_____

_____

_____

_____

Your Daily Lenten Checklist:

Did you accomplish it today?
Bravo! Put a check in the heart!

Daily Resolutions Fulfilled.............................. ♡

Spiritual Reading............................. ♡

Children's Activity............................ ♡

Daily Rosary............................ ♡
Additional Items:

_____ ♡

_____ ♡

Quote:

If we want to serve God, joy should be not only an element; it should be the staple of our life.

Our difficulties are so great, our enemies so many, that unless we are supported by joy, we shan't do what God wants us to do. It is a point of great consequence.

Rev. Daniel Considine, S.J., 1950's

Wednesday of the
Fourth Week in Lent

My Cross I Wish to
Thank God for Today:

_____

_____

The Person or Situation I am
Offering it for:

_____

_____

Something Special that Happened Today:

_____

_____

_____

_____

Your Daily Lenten Checklist:

Did you accomplish it today?
Bravo! Put a check in the heart!

Daily Resolutions Fulfilled...........................

Spiritual Reading................................

Children's Activity............................

Daily Rosary...........................
Additional Items

_____

_____

Quote:

Very few crosses are **DIRECTLY**
sent by God. God permits them, but
they come from someone, or
something else, or from ourselves -
being disappointed in something we
had aimed at. We should cut down
our estimate of what God really
sends us very considerably.

What does He want of me? He
wants you to take your life as it is,
bearing your trials and
disappointments as quietly as you
can. Empty lamenting over things
not being as they ought to be, must
be eschewed.

Rev. Daniel Considine, S.J., 1950's

Thursday of the Fourth Week in Lent

Three Things I am Grateful for Today:

1. _____

2. _____

3. _____

Something Special that Happened Today:

_____

_____

_____

_____

Your Daily Lenten Checklist:

Did you accomplish it today?
Bravo! Put a check in the heart!

Daily Resolutions Fulfilled............................ ♡

Spiritual Reading.................................... ♡

Children's Activity................................. ♡

Daily Rosary....................................... ♡
Additional Items:

_____ ♡

_____

Quote:

One of the ruses of the devil, whenever we fall short of the highest standard, is to tell us: 'You art not one of those chosen souls who are called to love God.'
You must think of Him as one who knows our poor craven natures. He knows it all seems flat and monotonous, and that you feel weary of well-doing. It will all pass: Our Lord hasn't abandoned you.
Rev. Daniel Considine, S.J., 1950's

Friday of the Fourth Week in Lent

Personal Prayer Intention for Today:

_____

_____

_____

Something Special that Happened Today:

_____

_____

_____

_____

Your Daily Lenten Checklist:

Did you accomplish it today? Bravo! Put a check in the heart!

Daily Resolutions Fulfilled.............................

Spiritual Reading.......................................

Children's Activity......................................

Daily Rosary..
Additional Items:

_____

_____

Quote:

"These diapers that are changed daily, these meals that are cooked again and again, these floors that are scrubbed today only to get dirty tomorrow — these are as truly prayer in a mother's vocation as the watches and prayers of the Religious are in theirs." -Mary Reed Newland, How to Raise Good Catholic Children

Saturday of the Fourth Week in Lent

My Cross I Wish to Thank God for Today:

_____

_____

The Person or Situation I am Offering it for:

_____

_____

_____

Something Special that Happened Today:

_____

_____

_____

_____

Your Daily Lenten Checklist:

Did you accomplish it today?
Bravo! Put a check in the heart!

Daily Resolutions Fulfilled.........................

Spiritual Reading................................

Children's Activity...........................

Daily Rosary...........................
Additional Items:

_____

_____

Quote:

It is amazing how, with time, the soul comes to dominate the body. Selfish people get the hard, selfish look. Generous people grow more physically attractive each day. People with the peace of God's friendship develop expressions that instantly attract and constantly charm. A mouth that speaks kindly becomes a beautiful mouth. Hands that serve generously become character-ful hands. Eyes that look out for affection on mankind are eyes that radiate an inner beauty not difficult to find. -Fr. Daniel A. Lord

Monday of Passion Week

Three Things I am Grateful for Today:

1. _____

2. _____

3. _____

Something Special that Happened Today:

_____

_____

_____

_____

Your Daily Lenten Checklist:

Did you accomplish it today?
Bravo! Put a check in the heart!

Daily Resolutions Fulfilled..........................

Spiritual Reading...............................

Children's Activity...........................

Daily Rosary.....................
Additional Items

_____

_____

Quote:

As women, wives and mothers we care so very much for our loved ones. We hurt when they hurt. Oftentimes we feel helpless.

We don't need to feel helpless. Let's take each nugget of suffering and, instead of kicking against the goad, give them to Our Lady, who, in turn, can polish them up, rid these nuggets of the dirt and grime of our self-love, and lay them at the feet of Our Lord as only His Mother can do.
-Leane VanderPutten

Tuesday of Passion Week

Personal Prayer Intention for Today:

_____

_____

_____

Something Special that Happened Today:

_____

_____

_____

_____

Your Daily Lenten Checklist:

Did you accomplish it today?
Bravo! Put a check in the heart!

Daily Resolutions Fulfilled.......................... ♡

Spiritual Reading.................................. ♡

Children's Activity................................ ♡

Daily Rosary.................................. ♡
Additional Items

_____ ♡

_____ ♡

Quote:

One day, we will see the influence of our own suffering well-borne on our little worlds.
Bishop Fulton Sheen once wrote "Pain, agony, disappointments, injustices-all these can be poured into a heavenly treasury from which the anemic, sinful, confused, ignorant souls may draw unto the healing of their wings."

Remember that in God's eyes, none of these sufferings are useless....they are nuggets...golden nuggets.
-Leane VanderPutten

Wednesday of Passion Week

My Cross I Wish to Thank God for Today:

_____

_____

The Person or Situation I am Offering it for:

_____

_____

Something Special that Happened Today:

_____

_____

_____

_____

Your Daily Lenten Checklist:

Did you accomplish it today?
Bravo! Put a check in the heart!

Daily Resolutions Fulfilled..........................

Spiritual Reading...............................

Children's Activity...........................

Daily Rosary............................
Additional Items

_____

_____

Quote:

Whatever you're going through today, whatever hardships you have during this Lenten season especially, take a moment to thank God for them. Give them as a gift to our suffering Lord. The light is always at the end of the tunnel and you don't want to be guilty for shaking your fist at God. This is one time you DO want to "jump the gun" and "count your chickens before they are hatched." You want to believe and KNOW that God is the Author of all and will turn this into good for you and for your family. You want to thank Him for your sufferings....

-Leane VanderPutten

Thursday of Passion Week

Three Things I am Grateful for Today:

1. _____
2. _____
3. _____

Something Special that Happened Today:

_____

_____

_____

_____

Your Daily Lenten Checklist:

Did you accomplish it today? Bravo! Put a check in the heart!

Daily Resolutions Fulfilled..........................

Spiritual Reading...............................

Children's Activity............................

Daily Rosary.............................
Additional Items:

_____

_____

Quote:

St. Thérèse used the expression: "I want everything that causes me difficulties." Externally it doesn't change anything about the situation, but interiorly it changes everything. This consent, inspired by love and trust, makes us free and active instead of passive, and enables God to draw good out of everything that happens to us whether good or bad.
-Fr. Jacques Philippe

Friday of Passion Week

Personal Prayer Intention for Today:

_____

_____

_____

Something Special that Happened Today:

_____

_____

_____

_____

Your Daily Lenten Checklist:

Did you accomplish it today?
Bravo! Put a check in the heart!

Daily Resolutions Fulfilled...........................

Spiritual Reading................................

Children's Activity................................

Daily Rosary...............................
Additional Items

_____

_____

Quote:

As often as you can during the day, recall your mind to the presence of God....Consider what God is doing, what you are doing. You will always find God's eyes fixed on you in unchangeable love.
We are rarely so taken up in our exchanges with others as to be unable from time to time to move our hearts into solitude with God.
-St. Francis de Sales

Saturday of Passion Week

My Cross I Wish to Thank God for Today:

_____

_____

The Person or Situation I am Offering it for:

_____

_____

Something Special that Happened Today:

_____

_____

_____

_____

Your Daily Lenten Checklist:

Did you accomplish it today?
Bravo! Put a check in the heart!

Daily Resolutions Fulfilled..........................

Spiritual Reading...

Children's Activity.......................................

Daily Rosary..
Additional Items

_____

_____

Quote:

How many opportunities do we, as wives and mothers, have each day to do God's will, not our own?? Many....many. We do not need a retreat to figure this out.

A wife and a mother's journey is laying down her life for those she loves. And we prove it each time we tend to the needs around us. We learn that most important life-lesson that the hermit in the desert is learning.....to lay down our lives for Christ.

-Leane VanderPutten

Holy Week!

As we receive the
blessed palm, let us
renew our pledge to
conquer with Jesus,
but let us not forget
that it was on the cross
that He conquered.
-Divine Intimacy

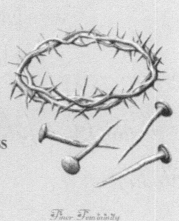

Finer Femininity

Jesus knew what was
awaiting Him, His heart was
tortured by it; and yet He not
only accepted but ardently
desired that hour, "His hour";
and He gave Himself into the
hands of His enemies with the
meekness of a lamb being led to
the slaughter.
-Divine Intimacy

Finer Femininity

"We cannot live a life
that will please Our
Lord — without
GREAT COST to
ourselves.
It is never an easy
thing, to be a GOOD
⚜ CATHOLIC. ⚜
An easy, self-
indulgent life — can
never be a CHRIST-
LIKE LIFE."

Finer Femininity

Monday of Holy Week

Three Things I am Grateful for Today:

1. _____

2. _____

3. _____

Something Special that Happened Today:

_____

_____

_____

_____

Your Daily Lenten Checklist:

Did you accomplish it today?
Bravo! Put a check in the heart!

Daily Resolutions Fulfilled...........................

Spiritual Reading.............................

Children's Activity...........................

Daily Rosary...........................
Additional Items:

_____

_____

Quote:

Often turn to Our Lord, Who is watching you, poor frail little being that you are, amid your labors and distractions. He sends you help and blesses your afflictions. This thought should enable you to bear your troubles patiently and quietly, for love of Him Who only allows you to be tried for your own good.
Raise your heart continually to God, seek His aid, and let the foundation of your consolation be your happiness in being His.
All vexations and annoyances will be powerless to move you while you remember that you have such a Friend – such a Stay, such a Refuge.
-St. Francis de Sales

Tuesday of Holy Week

Personal Prayer Intention for Today:

_____

_____

_____

Something Special that Happened Today:

_____

_____

_____

_____

Your Daily Lenten Checklist:

Did you accomplish it today?
Bravo! Put a check in the heart!

Daily Resolutions Fulfilled............................ ♡

Spiritual Reading.............................. ♡

Children's Activity............................ ♡

Daily Rosary.............................. ♡
Additional Items

_____

_____

Quote:

Like Christ, we bend our hearts down to the lowly, the little ones. We wipe away tears, change diapers, put on band-aids, feed the hungry and many other menial, yet meaningful services. We attune ourselves to the powerless, not the powerful.

So, take heart, dear Ladies, as this season of Lent progresses and you find yourselves stumbling to accomplish the fasts and penances you set out to accomplish. Remember, our life is already one of very special sacrifice. Let's work on making the sacrifice more beautiful for Our Lord.....less complaining, more cheerfulness, more offering our hearts to Our Lord during the day.

Leane VanderPutten

Wednesday of Holy Week

My Cross I Wish to Thank God for Today:

_____

_____

The Person or Situation I am Offering it for:

_____

_____

Something Special that Happened Today:

_____

_____

_____

_____

Your Daily Lenten Checklist:

Did you accomplish it today?
Bravo! Put a check in the heart!

Daily Resolutions Fulfilled.............................. ♡

Spiritual Reading.............................. ♡

Children's Activity.............................. ♡

Daily Rosary.............................. ♡
Additional Items

_____ ♡

_____ ♡

Quote:

Always act patiently and answer graciously. That it takes the "patience of an angel" to rule vigilantly over the little world of the family is beyond question. Affability is essential.
By goodwill you will gain hearts and souls without exception.
Loving much is the key to gain all.
-Fr. Raoul Plus, S.J., Christ in the Home, 1950's

Holy Thursday

Three Things I am Grateful for Today:

1. _____

2. _____

3. _____

Something Special that Happened Today:

_____

_____

_____

_____

Your Daily Lenten Checklist:

Did you accomplish it today?
Bravo! Put a check in the heart!

Daily Resolutions Fulfilled...................... ♡

Spiritual Reading................................. ♡

Children's Activity.............................. ♡

Daily Rosary..................................... ♡
Additional Items

_____ ♡

_____ ♡

Quote:

The Gospel of this day tells of the lesson Jesus gave us in brotherly love and humility as He first washed the feet of His disciples. We, wives and mothers, are given a special vocation of love and service. We are, as Christ, to "wash the feet" of those in our charge by being available in each moment of each day to tend to their needs.
-Leane VanderPutten

Good Friday

Personal Prayer Intention for Today:

_____

_____

_____

Something Special that Happened Today:

_____

_____

_____

_____

Your Daily Lenten Checklist:

Did you accomplish it today?
Bravo! Put a check in the heart!

Daily Resolutions Fulfilled............................

Spiritual Reading.....................................

Children's Activity...................................

Daily Rosary...
Additional Items:

_____

_____

Quote:

O Christ, Son of God, as I contemplate the great sufferings You endured for us on the Cross, I hear You saying to my soul: 'It is not in jest that I have loved you!'
-Divine Intimacy

Holy Saturday

My Cross I Wish to
Thank God for Today:

_____

_____

The Person or Situation I am
Offering it for:

_____

_____

Something Special that Happened Today:

_____

_____

_____

_____

Your Daily Lenten Checklist:

Did you accomplish it today?
Bravo! Put a check in the heart!

Daily Resolutions Fulfilled..........................

Spiritual Reading..............................

Children's Activity..........................

Daily Rosary.........................
Additional Items

_____

_____

Quote:

The truth is that life and
everything in life are merely
means to an end, to a purpose, to
an achievement. And the
achievement is nothing short of
an eternity of such happiness as
cannot possibly be described
because it is far beyond the power
of the human mind to realize or
to imagine.
-The Family and the Cross, Joseph
Breig, 1950's

Easter Morning. Alleluia!

The Hallel, greatest of Hebrew expressions of praise, together with Jah, the shortened form of Jahve, God's name, combine to make this lovely word.
Dom Winzen writes:"On the eve of Septuagesima Sunday, the Alleluia was buried. Now it rises out of the tomb..". The Alleluia is the heart of the Opus Dei; the song which the Moses of the New Testament sings together with His People after He has passed through the Red Sea of His Death into the glory of His Resurrection.
The first child awake races downstairs! Quickly they all gather and at last the door to the living room is opened.
There are the marvelous baskets, resplendent with decorations, with gifts, with goodies. Walk carefully. The eggs are hidden everywhere.
All together sing another Alleluia! as the early one lights the Paschal candle.
Then to Mass, to the great joy of Easter Communion. He is in each of us; therefore we are one in Him.
At every Mass, He will be our Paschal Lamb, the perfect sacrifice, the perfect Victim, offered everywhere for us, always, until the world comes to an end.
Home to the beautiful breakfast table, the delicious Easter bread, the excitement of the egg hunt, and the opening of gifts.
It has been so long since we have sung Alleluia after Grace. What a glorious morning!
The Paschal candle is lighted. While we rejoice, it burns with a steady flame. It says, "I am risen, and am still with thee, Alleluia!"
-Mary Reed Newland, The Year and Our Children

And He departed from our sight that we might return to our heart, and there find Him. For He departed, and behold, He is here.
-St. Augustine

Like the holy women, we, too, have a keen desire to find the Lord; perhaps we have been seeking Him for many long years. Sustained by His grace, Divine Providence has helped us roll away many stones, overcome many difficulties. Nevertheless, the search for God is progressive, and must be maintained during our whole life.
Divine Intimacy

About the Author

Mrs. Leane VanderPutten lives in rural Kansas with her husband of over 30 years.

She is the mother and grandmother of 11 children and 23 grandchildren....and growing.

They are devoted to Tradition within the Fold of the Cahtolic Church, homeschoolers, with 5 children still at home.

Their family life is lively, full of faith and joy!

Made in the USA
Monee, IL
17 December 2020